Bereavement

Bereavement

Jean Watson

Text copyright © Jean Watson 2005
The author asserts the moral right
to be identified as the author of this work

Published by
The Bible Reading Fellowship
15 The Chambers
Abingdon, OX14 3FE
United Kingdom
Tel: +44 (0)1865 319700
Email: enquiries@brf.org.uk
Website: www.brf.org.uk
BRF is a Registered Charity

ISBN 978 0 85746 326 5
First published 2005, reprinted twice
This edition 2015
All rights reserved

Acknowledgements
Scripture quotations are taken from the Holy Bible, New International Version, copyright © 1973, 1978, 1984 by International Bible Society, are used by permission of Hodder & Stoughton Publishers, a division of Hodder Headline Ltd. All rights reserved. 'NIV' is a registered trademark of International Bible Society. UK trademark number 1448790.

p. 14: Quotation from Dale and Juanita Ryan, *Rooted in God's Love*, IVP, 1992.
p. 16: Quotation from Colin Murray Parkes, *All in the End is Harvest*, ed. A. Whitaker, DLT, 1984.
p. 18: Quotation from Joseph Bayly, *The View from a Hearse*, D.C. Cook Publishing Company, 1973.
p. 23: Quotation from Dick Keyes, *Beyond Identity*, Servant Books, 1984.
p. 27: Quotation from Frederick Buechner, *Telling Secrets*, HarperCollins, 1991.

Cover photograph: © Iani Barbitta/Gettyimages

Every effort has been made to trace and contact copyright owners for material used in this resource. We apologise for any inadvertent omissions or errors, and would ask those concerned to contact us so that full acknowledgement can be made in the future.

A catalogue record for this book is available from the British Library

Printed in the UK by Rainbow Print

Introduction

My heart goes out to anyone who has lost a loved one. This book is for you. I wrote the first edition some years after my husband's sudden, untimely death. Since then there have been more bereavements in my family—those of my elderly father and mother after their long, slow, sad declines and that of my sister-in-law from a tragic form of dementia contracted while she was in her 50s. Those four bereavements and losses were very different from one another and were differently experienced by everyone involved, depending on our relationship with the deceased, and on our own unique personalities and situations.

The loss of a beloved person—family member or dear friend—is the main focus in this little book but I know that there are many other varieties of bereavement and loss which disrupt people's lives and cause emotional pain: the death of a pet; the loss of a job; having to uproot from loved people and places; life-threatening or life-limiting illness or disability.

In one of the best books I have read on suffering, now sadly out of print, Peter Kreeft writes: 'We lose little bits of life daily—our health, our strength, our youth, our hopes, our dreams, our friends, our children, our lives—all these dribble away like water through our desperate, shaking fingers.' He adds: 'The only hearts that do not break are the ones that are busily constructing little hells of loveless control, cocoons of safe, respectable selfishness to insulate themselves against the tidal wave of tears that comes sooner or later' (*Making Sense Out of Suffering*, Hodder & Stoughton, 1986).

That said, I would like to add that there is hope and help for us as we encounter life's traumas, pain and losses. While it's true that there are differences in the way people experience these, there do also seem to be emotions and landmarks which are common to many, and I focused on some of these when I wrote the first edition of this book. I believe this material is still helpful and relevant now as I write this introduction to the new edition.

The process of grieving and mourning is helped when you find you can identify with what other people have felt and thought; it is even helped when your response is along the lines of: 'No, that's not how it is for me. My feelings/thoughts are like this…' 'Good' grief is about being totally real about who and where you are in your pain and trauma; 'good' mourning is about processing your feelings, thoughts and experiences, in private and with a friend or friends you can trust, until they become an accepted part of yourself and of your past, present and ongoing story.

If you are hurting, I hope and pray that you will be supported as you find your own pathway through grief. If you are wanting to get alongside someone else as they grieve and mourn, I hope and pray that you will have or develop the necessary understanding and sensitivity.

GENESIS 49:33

A thousand doors

When Jacob had finished giving instructions to his sons, he drew his feet up into the bed, breathed his last and was gathered to his people.

Jacob died after a long life, having said and done all he wanted to and being surrounded by family and friends. But that's certainly not everyone's experience. As Philip Massinger, living in the 16th century, wrote, 'Death has a thousand doors to let out life.'

If you have been bereaved, I wonder by which 'door' death entered to take away the person you loved. If our loved ones live to a ripe old age and die peacefully, or if death brings an end to their suffering, we can be pleased for them, however sadly we miss them. Our feelings are very different if death comes in a way that we find devastating—as a result of a crime, an accident or neglect, for instance.

Because my husband's death during surgery was so unexpected, an inquest proved necessary and this returned a verdict of 'death by misadventure'. Shock and unreality gripped me. I remember thinking and saying out loud many times something like, 'This can't and shouldn't have happened—but it has. I can't believe it, but I must.'

Perhaps you are feeling numb and even wanting to stay that way so as to block out the unacceptable events. Opening up to a trusted friend, or getting our feelings down on paper, can be ways of helping us 'get real' about how our loved one died.

Lord of all the doors of life and death, I come to you, just as I am...

PSALM 31:9–10

Waves of pain

Be merciful to me, O Lord, for I am in distress; my eyes grow weak with sorrow, my soul and my body with grief. My life is consumed by anguish and my years by groaning; my strength fails because of my affliction, and my bones grow weak.

What words or phrases express the psalmist's feelings? He was in distress, grief, anguish; he felt weak, overwhelmed, worn out: he experienced physical and psychological pain.

Bereaved people at different times have come up with an enormous variety of words to describe how they feel: numb, unreal, disorientated, shattered, heartbroken, alone, angry, empty, hopeless, purposeless, vulnerable, insecure, inadequate, churned up, relieved that the suffering and strain are over...

C.S. Lewis also identified fear, weariness and a sense of waiting for something to happen. For me, this feeling that life was on hold had a double aspect. There was the desperate hope that life would return to pre-bereavement normality and, paradoxically, the dread realisation that it wouldn't, *ever*—indeed, that the next terrible thing was only a phone call, letter or ring at the doorbell away.

Some people may even start to wonder whether they are going mad; others may not feel quite so battered by their emotions. Either way, I am sure that what you are experiencing is quite normal. Facing our feelings— all of them, however painful and troubling they are—is a necessary part of 'good' grief, 'healthy' mourning. Only so can we recover and grow.

But that's jumping ahead; for now, it's a matter of weathering those waves of pain moment by moment, drawing on all the inner and outer resources we can muster.

Jesus, could it really be true that my pain is your pain (Isaiah 53:4)? Help, Lord!

MATTHEW 5:4; ECCLESIASTES 3:1, 4b

Maps of mourning

Blessed are those who mourn, for they will be comforted.

There is… a time to mourn.

I was given these words from Matthew 5:4 in a sympathy card and at first my response was, 'If given a choice, I'd rather be unblessed and not mourning—thanks very much.' Later on, I thought long and hard about the kind of mourning that led to being comforted.

Different words and images are used to convey mourning: a process, a journey, a rollercoaster ride (without the fun), a tunnel, an illness… and each probably contributes something to our understanding of the experience.

Some people find it helpful to identify stages in what might be considered good, healthy mourning. One map of mourning, if I can put it like that, highlights the following: shock; yearning and searching; withdrawel and apathy; anger and protest; the phase of mitigation—a kind of finding; the gradual gaining of a new identity. A chaplain who worked in a hospice and home of healing identifies four main watersheds: unreality—'I don't believe it'; reality—'I can't bear it'; adjustment—'What can I do to handle it?'; and moving on—'I feel better but I'll never feel the same again'.

These and any other models should never be set in concrete. Not everyone experiences the same sort or sequence of 'stages'. Shock and denial are more usual in the earlier days and weeks after death, but they can also occur before death—when the diagnosis was first learnt, for instance.

Our progress through mourning is likely to be back and forth and up and down. But as long as we are moving in the right direction, things will get better.

Lord, this is where I feel I am in my mourning…

JOHN 11:33–36; 1 SAMUEL 1:15–16

Grief is personal

When Jesus saw [Mary] weeping, and the Jews who had come along with her also weeping, he was deeply moved in spirit and troubled. 'Where have you laid [Lazarus]?' he asked. 'Come and see, Lord,' they replied. Jesus wept. Then the Jews said, 'See how he loved him!'

Hannah replied, '… I have been praying here out of my great anguish and grief.'

In our first passage, Mary and Jesus wept together, and Jesus was also 'deeply moved in spirit and troubled' over the untimely death of a loved one.

We have a right, indeed a need, to be ourselves in our grieving. We do not have to hold back our natural responses and try to react as others have done or as we have been told that we should. I sometimes want to say to bereaved people, 'You don't need to be "strong"—you just need to be real.' But maybe for some, being strong is being real. And even if, for others, it is not, they will need to become aware of this for themselves.

Some of us, like Hannah, more spontaneous and open by temperament, may abandon ourselves to grief in a very intense, vociferous way. Others, more reserved, may prefer to mourn more privately, allowing only a few close friends in, and carrying on fairly normally to all outward appearances. And there will be all kinds of variations on those responses.

When Hannah let herself go in her grief, an initially judgemental priest turned into a sympathetic well-wisher. Mary had Jesus close by, feeling for and with her. Who is alongside you?

Has some aspect of your grieving surprised you? What might it be 'telling' you? Do you need a friend to help you unpack this?

Friday

JOB 23:3; JOHN 20:11a, 13b, 15

Yearning

'If only I knew where to find him.'

Mary stood outside the tomb crying... 'They have taken my Lord away,' she said, 'and I don't know where they have put him.' ... 'Woman,' [Jesus] said, 'why are you crying? Who is it you are looking for?' Thinking he was the gardener, she said, 'Sir, if you have carried him away, tell me where you have put him, and I will get him.'

Where are you? This poignant question is often on our hearts, if not actually on our lips, during the early days of our bereavement. In the first verse, Job is speaking of his anguished yearning to find and question God, but the same yearning can be directed towards the loved ones we have lost.

In the second passage, Mary doesn't actually ask, 'Where are you?' but that is what her heart is crying out. All she wants is to find Jesus and see him again. She knows, or thinks she does, what has happened to him, but the longing to see him again brings her to his tomb. Like Mary, we too know that our loved ones have died, but we may still feel the need to 'search' for them, and we certainly yearn to see them again. I remember pleading with God, 'Just let me have him back for five minutes so I can say goodbye and hug him and tell him that I love him.'

This yearning is very normal—and very painful. If we face and feel it, it will recede in time, as our loved one becomes part of us in spirit and in memory. Poet Brian Patten writes, 'A man lives for as long as we carry him inside us' ('So many different lengths of time'). Our Christian hope is that our loved one is with God—and hence alive in a different and far more lasting way in that dimension too.

Lord, make the Christian hope real to me again...

GENESIS 37:34–35

Absence and loneliness

Jacob tore his clothes, put on sackcloth and mourned for his son many days. All his sons and daughters came to comfort him, but he refused to be comforted. 'No,' he said, 'in mourning will I go down to the grave to my son.' So his father wept for him.

Bereavement makes us feel so alone and so vulnerable: we have been amputated from our other (and perhaps we might feel we want to add, our better) half. And in this state we have to face not just our own tasks but also those that our loved one used to do for us or with us.

Day by day, sights, sounds, smells, tastes, tasks and situations will underline our loss and aloneness. Each 'never again' thought is sheer anguish. We will never again share a joke, go to bed, watch a sunset, make toast, go for a walk, have a holiday… *together*.

After about six years I was able to find the word to express what I was missing the most, and this was being *cherished*, as I had been by my husband and would never be again.

We need both privacy and close friends so that we can cry, talk, pray, and whatever else we must do, until we accept and feel the pain of every aspect of our aloneness and our loved one's absence.

As the years pass, significant dates keep coming up: wedding and other anniversaries, birthdays and holidays. Each one gives us the opportunity to face up to sad memories, or to happy ones now tinged with the pain of loss; and to the prospect of living with mingled joy and sadness in the years ahead.

Can you share with God and a friend how alone and vulnerable you feel and what you are missing the most?

2 SAMUEL 18:33

Unfinished business

The king [David] was shaken. He went up to the room over the gateway and wept. As he went, he said: 'O my son Absalom! My son, my son Absalom! If only I had died instead of you—O Absalom, my son, my son!'

If our relationship with the person who died was basically happy and harmonious, our pain will at least be free of the kind of regret and remorse that occur when things like misunderstanding and conflict were never resolved.

Absalom rebelled against his father, David, and tried to take the kingdom from him. David's feelings of grief after Absalom's death would have reflected that conflict. He must have been torn apart at the way their relationship had gone wrong. Perhaps he blamed himself for some of the problems, and he would surely have wished that he'd had the chance to say something loving and forgiving to Absalom before the end.

What can we do in similar situations where, for example, death occurs suddenly, snatching away our opportunity to say to or hear from our loved one words such as 'I love you', 'I forgive you', 'Please forgive me', or 'Goodbye'?

Some people have been helped by writing letters as if to their deceased loved one, saying what they wished they had said face-to-face. Where there's anger and the feeling of having been unjustly treated, some have found it helpful to write it all down and then, when ready, write FORGIVEN across the words. Afterwards the relevant page can be kept or destroyed. Prayer, sharing with a wise and trusted friend, going to our loved one's grave or memorial and 'talking'—these can also help to bring relief and closure.

Lord, I desperately need to forgive/to be and feel forgiven. Help me to draw on the love, humility and grace that will make this possible.

Tuesday

JOB 29:1–2, 4–6

Cries and questions

Job continued… 'How I long for the months gone by, for the days when God watched over me…! Oh, for the days when I was in my prime, when God's intimate friendship blessed my house, when the Almighty was still with me and my children were around me, when my path was drenched with cream and the rock poured out for me streams of olive oil.'

Job, in his anguish, looks back to a time in his life when he had everything going for him—home and family, health and wealth. The conclusion he draws is that God was pleased with him then, but isn't any more. It's the wrong conclusion, but for now let's stay with the feelings.

Help! I am adrift, lost—save me! Where are you? What have I done? Why are you angry with me? Where were you when my loved one died? Where are you when 'bad' things and natural disasters happen to children and to 'good' and 'bad' people alike? If you're in charge, why don't you do something? If you're not, what hope is there for anyone? What do your presence and help really mean? And what has prayer to do with any of it?

The psalmists tell us to pour out our hearts before God (Psalm 62:8), but they also ask why God is distant and hides himself in times of trouble (Psalm 10:1). Hurt, anger, desperation, bewilderment: can you identify with these feelings? And what happens when we bring such feelings to God?

Reflecting the experience of many, Dale and Juanita Ryan wrote, 'God, who may have seemed so present and attentive when our pain was less intense, can seem strangely absent just when we need him most.'

Lord, where are you? Please, now, soon, reach out to me in some way—through someone I meet, something I see, do, read or remember.

Wednesday

Taking care of ourselves

David pleaded with God for the child. He fasted and went into his house and spent the nights lying on the ground... David noticed that his servants were whispering among themselves and he realised the child was dead... Then David got up from the ground. After he had washed, put on lotions and changed his clothes, he went into the house of the Lord and worshipped. Then he went to his own house, and at his request they served him food, and he ate.

While his baby was alive, David fasted and prayed. He thought about nothing else, neglecting his own needs. After the baby had died, however, he got up, washed, changed his clothes, ate food and worshipped God.

Now I'm not suggesting that we should accept and recover from tragedy as quickly as David appears to have done, but I do think there are ways in which we can help ourselves in times of distress. David helped himself in two important ways. He faced reality—he accepted that his son had died; and then he took care of himself and his needs.

Now that our loved one has gone, we may feel of little account. This is where true friends can help us to feel valuable in our own right, by caring for us and including us. Their attitude can remind us of what we believe about God's valuing of us as an individual. In bereavement we often feel disabled, both emotionally and physically, so we may need to be selective about what we read, listen to, view; to give ourselves easier agendas; to pay attention to our need for rest, relaxation, sleep and perhaps medication.

Spend a little time reflecting in God's presence on your mind, body and emotions. Are they 'telling' you about needs you have been ignoring and need to address?

PSALM 77:5–6a, 11–12

Positive focus

I thought about the former days, the years of long ago; I remembered my songs in the night… I will remember the deeds of the Lord; yes, I will remember your miracles of long ago. I will meditate on all your works and consider all your mighty deeds.

In grieving, our focus, necessarily, is on sadness and suffering, but we need to be ready to adjust to a less one-sided view of reality when the time is right for us.

One way of doing this is by making the most of our good memories. The psalmist remembered the good things in the past and recognised that these came, ultimately, from God. Yes, there will be sadness in remembering what once was and is no more, but also joy and thankfulness; and in looking back we can also become aware of good things which haven't been swept away and which we could still be enjoying, at least in memory.

What other 'positive focus' attitudes and actions are there? We can give ourselves permission to enjoy life and to laugh again—and then spend time with the people, books, films and activities that will help us to do that. We can learn to live a day at a time and appreciate the small joys and assets that we didn't take much notice of before. We can keep trusting that we will feel better; indeed, that we will learn and grow and emerge with new insights, qualities and skills for enriching our own and other people's lives.

In the words of Colin Murray Parkes, 'Our aim cannot be to cancel out the past, to try and forget, but to ensure that the strength and meaning which gave beauty to the old pattern is remembered and reinterpreted in the pattern now emerging.'

Spend some time in God's presence, remembering thankfully all that was good in the past and identifying with joy all that is good in the present.

Friday

RUTH 1:20b–21a; EPHESIANS 4:31–32

Traps for the unwary

'Call me Mara, because the Almighty has made my life very bitter. I went away full, but the Lord has brought me back empty.'

Get rid of all bitterness, rage and anger, brawling and slander, along with every form of malice. Be kind and compassionate to one another, forgiving each other, just as in Christ God forgave you.

In the first verses, Naomi's feelings and words are totally understandable to anyone who has suffered one major loss, let alone three bereavements—a husband and two sons. But it wasn't the Almighty who had made her life bitter. Bitterness is a response that we choose or a reaction we reject. We have no control over some of what happens to us, but we can choose our attitudes and actions in relation to them.

The other verses identify some unhelpful and helpful ways of responding to people and events, leading to either negativity and stagnation or learning and growth. Among the former, I would include wanting revenge, blaming and scapegoating, settling for permanent victim status, choosing harmful 'distractions' or making useful ones a way of life rather than temporary relief.

Also, when feeling vulnerable, we can be prone to self-pity and resentment. It's important to treat as a bonus, not a right, every single good thing that is given to us, and to stay open to other people's situations and needs. Our friends are not responsible for our situation and they cannot meet all our expectations, least of all give us the one thing we most desperately want—our loved one alive and well and back with us again.

Lord, show me where my attitudes are harming myself or others.

JOB 2:11a, 13; ROMANS 12:15b

Love with skin on

Job's three friends... sat on the ground with him for seven days and seven nights. No one said a word to him, because they saw how great his suffering was.

Mourn with those who mourn.

As many people have pointed out, Job's three friends did far more good by sitting on the ground with him for seven days and saying nothing than they did with all their subsequent dogmatic and judgemental speeches. Their initial restraint and sensitivity exemplified aspects of empathy. This can be described as love with skin on—love made visible and tangible by attitudes, actions and words, conveying respect and understanding, support and care. Such love sets grieving people free to be themselves, tell their stories, share their emotions and thoughts.

How do you feel about receiving help from others? What do you still need? Is there any way in which you could find it, ask for it, make it available? As well as family and friends, acquaintances and strangers made it on to my list of likely or unlikely 'angels' from whom I received practical or emotional support—whether in some major way or through a kind word said or helping hand offered at just the right moment.

Echoing the experience of many others, Joseph Bayly wrote, 'I was sitting torn by grief. Someone came and talked to me... He talked constantly. He said things I knew were true. I was unmoved except to wish that he would go away... Another came and sat beside me. He didn't talk... He just sat beside me for an hour or more, listened when I said something, answered briefly, prayed simply. Left. I was moved, I was comforted. I hated to see him go.'

Lord, thank you for my comforters...

JOB 6:14–15, 21, 26; PSALM 38:11

Cold comfort

A despairing man should have the devotion of his friends... But my brothers are as undependable as intermittent streams...You too have proved to be of no help; you see something dreadful and are afraid... Do you mean to correct what I say, and treat the words of a despairing man as wind?

My friends and companions avoid me because of my wounds; my neighbours stay far away.

Job's friends give us a classic example of cold comfort, and Job replies in effect, 'With friends like you, who needs enemies? What has happened to me has frightened you and you are reacting to that rather than responding to my needs—correcting me rather than empathising with me in my despair.'

Job's friends were judgemental, jumped to conclusions and gave unwanted advice. David's friends, in the second passage, avoided him—something many still do to bereaved people, as though they had an infectious disease, at a time when they really need company and companionship.

Then there is the 'buck up—other people have it worse' attitude. A friend still grieving over the death of her young baby was treated by a relative to accounts of atrocities elsewhere. In our pain, the last thing we need are stories of other people's illnesses, losses, disasters; or indeed of their 'healings' and triumphant faith. Trying to shame or shock grieving people into getting their personal tragedy into 'perspective' is insensitive and counterproductive; mourners need acceptance and support to enable them to reflect, learn, grow and move on in their own time and way.

Lord Jesus, are you weeping with me, as you wept at the grave of Lazarus? I trust that you are—and it helps; thank you.

Tuesday

SONG OF SONGS 2:11–13a; JOB 38:4a, 6–7

Wonderful world

See! The winter is past; the rains are over and gone. Flowers appear on the earth; the season of singing has come, the cooing of doves is heard in our land. The fig tree forms its early fruit; the blossoming vines spread their fragrance.

Where were you when I laid the earth's foundation? ... On what were its footings set... while the morning stars sang together and all the angels shouted for joy?

These verses speak of nature's beauty, order and harmony, and hint at its potential for evoking joy. In early bereavement, all that loveliness, interconnection and continuity may strike us as heartless and add to our pain and sense of isolation. Later, we can find these same aspects of the world about us reassuring, delightful and fascinating in their own right, and, more especially, as gifts arising from God's creative love.

A new desire to play our part in taking care of the environment often follows. Many people develop green fingers or get involved with environmental projects or take up landscape painting or some other form of creativity in celebration of our wonderful world.

One way or another, being reconnected with nature can help us to recover from and grow through times of trauma.

Could you allow more time in your life for reconnecting with sun and rain, sea and earth, living and growing things; and for learning more about God's nature and ways through creation?

ISAIAH 43:2A; 45:3a

Promises and presence

When you pass through the waters, I will be with you; and when you pass through the rivers, they will not sweep over you... I will give you the treasures of darkness, riches stored in secret places, so that you may know that I am the Lord.

Some people find God's promises a great strength to them all through their bereavement. Others admit that scripture verses meant little while they were overwhelmed by anguish, whereas the loving presence of people did touch them.

Remember the Papa Panov story? A shoemaker waited all Christmas Day for a promised visit from Jesus. Instead, various needy people came his way and he helped them, giving away the gifts that he had put aside for Jesus. At the end of the day, Papa Panov was desperately disappointed, but then he seemed to see all the people he had helped and they were saying, 'Didn't you see me, Papa Panov?' And another voice told him that what he had done for those in need, he had done for him—and he finally got the message that Jesus had indeed come to visit him.

We can be Jesus' hands, feet and heart for others and they can be the same for us. Yes, God works through prayer, Bible reading and church services, but he also, especially during hard times, 'comes' to us, 'speaks' to us and 'touches' us through people and the world about us. God's immanence, vulnerability and closeness in these ways can be a real 'treasure of darkness' to us as we grieve.

Are you seeing new aspects of God through people and the world about you? Could these be some of your 'treasures of darkness'—gems or insights or nuggets of truth mined during your time of pain and difficulty?

Thursday

1 TIMOTHY 6:17b; LAMENTATIONS 3:22–23

Life goes on

God… richly provides us with everything for our enjoyment.

Because of the Lord's great love we are not consumed, for his compassions never fail. They are new every morning; great is your faithfulness.

'Life goes on.' People use this phrase so glibly. For those who have been bereaved, it is fraught with ambiguity.

Life goes on all around us while our life is in ruins, or so it may feel. Life goes on while our motivation and energy are very low. There are people to inform about what has happened, and that's painful. There are those who visit and bring gifts, which is wonderful, but it's sometimes hard to summon up the energy to respond to their generosity as we would wish to. On top of that, there are the church services to sort out, legal matters to attend to, decisions to be made—and the rest!

Life goes on, and some aspects of this can feel, particularly at first, like an affront. Our hearts are breaking, but flowers bloom and trees blossom and newsreaders switch their smiles back on and report on something utterly trivial, having just conveyed what represents an appalling tragedy for someone, somewhere.

Life goes on, and some aspects of this can benefit us right from the start. I'm thinking of the regular events and routines that give our days structure and a sense of continuity. Our eyes are opened to these and other little blessings that we hardly noticed or appreciated before.

Ponder in God's presence on any aspects of life's ongoingness that are a blessing to you. Early snowdrops and all the other perennials that survive our neglect? Much-loved people, books and films that are still 'there' for us? The endless fascination of the changing skies? A happy child at play?

Friday

PSALM 23:1a, 4, 6

Perspective

The Lord is my shepherd... Even though I walk through the valley of the shadow of death, I will fear no evil, for you are with me; your rod and your staff, they comfort me... Surely goodness and love will follow me all the days of my life, and I will dwell in the house of the Lord for ever.

One day we will feel ready to step back a bit so as to gain perspective on our bereavement—and I must stress that it is up to us to know when that time comes, not for someone else to tell us when they think it is.

One context we can consider, when we are ready to do so, is that of the rest of our lives. It is helpful to see life as a continuum. A big event, whether it's a great triumph or a great tragedy, is an important part of one's life but not the whole of it; each event needs to be integrated into our past and future story. One way in which I tried to gain this kind of perspective was by reflecting on 'What I have lost', 'What I have not lost', and 'What I have gained'.

We can gain perspective, too, through setting our story in the context of other people's stories, making comparisons both upwards and downwards—with those more battered by life's pain and injustice than we are, as well as with those who seem to be having a ball. Widening the canvas to take in the whole picture gives us yet another context in which to place our own story. Dick Keyes uses the phrase 'master story', which he defines as 'some kind of picture of what the world is like and how it works'. He continues, 'In the light of this story we interpret the meaning of our lives.' In Psalm 23 David was placing his life in this ultimate context. Does it help us to do the same with ours?

The Lord is my...? David finished that sentence with the word 'shepherd'. That was his master story or picture—in brief. What is yours?

23

ECCLESIASTES 3:1a, 4

Time heals—or does it?

There is a time for everything… a time to weep and a time to laugh, a time to mourn and a time to dance.

From reflecting and talking to others, I believe that time on its own doesn't automatically heal. A situation can fester and get worse. Emotional healing only happens if the factors conducive to it are present along with time.

For a start, we need to want to recover. It is possible for people to get stuck as 'bereaved' or even 'ill' and to want to remain in that 'special' category, exempting them from engaging robustly with life and people ever again. Given wise and caring support, people can be helped to regain trust and courage, to see that recovering and being happy again would be a tribute to rather than a betrayal of their loved one.

Wanting to recover needs to be implemented by our choices and actions. Crucially, we need to face our situation and pain. It's easier to feel angry than sad, so it could be tempting to opt for 'bereavement rage' or for constant 'driven' activity, but going through the grief is the only genuine way forward.

What else is involved in recovery, growth and the creation of a new life? Making the most of our memories, for one thing; and accepting the practical and emotional help we need, for another. Also required will be determination and effort as well as courage, honesty and humility.

Only in that kind of a context does time heal, or so I believe. As to how much time—that will vary from person to person and situation to situation.

Spend time in God's presence, reflecting on where you are in your journey through grief.

JOB 10:3, 8; 13:24

Faith—lost or changing?

Does it please you to oppress me, to spurn the work of your hands, while you smile on the schemes of the wicked? … Your hands shaped me and made me. Will you now turn and destroy me? … Why do you hide your face and consider me your enemy?

Job, speaking out of a strong sense of hurt and injustice, is basically telling God and his judgemental friends that they have got it wrong. Yes, he knows he isn't perfect, but he also knows that he didn't deserve the catalogue of catastrophes that have befallen him. Why is God treating him like that and letting wicked people get away with their wickedness? Does God want to destroy him? Why won't God let him state his case—why is he hiding from him?

When tragedy strikes at us personally, our responses can be very similar to Job's. We too know we're not perfect, but that doesn't explain what has happened to us. Why doesn't God do something about, or even just explain, the seemingly random distribution of life's injustices?

At first our own inner distress and clamour make it impossible for us to hear any 'answers' to such questions. Later, though, our hearing can improve! I had it confirmed to me that there are no pat answers to life's deeper questions and mysteries. I also realised that what cannot be understood intellectually can be lived with; that 'lost' faith can be found again, albeit amended and refined; and that bereavement can usher in a new stage of our spiritual life—one in which we have the opportunity to dig deeper for life's more paradoxical meanings, and hence to learn and grow in new ways.

Sharing our doubts and dilemmas with God is an act of honest faith.

Tuesday

ISAIAH 53:3–5; 2 CORINTHIANS 1:3–4

Wounder and healer

He was... a man of sorrows, and familiar with suffering... Surely he took up our infirmities and carried our sorrows... By his wounds we are healed.

God... who comforts us in all our troubles, so that we can comfort those in any trouble with the comfort we ourselves have received from God.

As all bereaved people realise, love is paradoxically both the greatest wounder and the best healer—the love and care of others, including very crucially that of our loved one. The memories and tangible evidence of my husband's love, along with the emotional and practical support that I was receiving from family and friends, were what kept me going at the very worst times. They gradually enabled me to make the choices and take the steps that brought me through grief and into recovering and making a life for myself.

And what of God's perfect love? I trusted in my head that it was there for me, but it was people's love that brought its warmth to my heart and life again. Love from its divine source, mediated through others, can give us courage to opt back—perhaps rather warily at first—into the ups and downs of close relationships. For though a love-free zone might be to some extent a pain-free zone, it lacks joy and all the other 'treasures' of genuine friendship and intimacy that give value and meaning to our lives.

Lord, I want to be courageous enough to keep growing in my capacity to receive and reflect genuine love—love that never gives up hope or gives up trying; love that is always present when needed to empathise and comfort.

ISAIAH 40:31; JAMES 3:17

Wise strength

Those who hope in the Lord will renew their strength. They will soar on wings like eagles; they will run and not grow weary, they will walk and not be faint.

The wisdom that comes from heaven is first of all pure; then peace-loving, considerate, submissive, full of mercy and good fruit, impartial and sincere.

You may often feel, as I do, very weak, ineffective and lacking in wisdom. But this may not be the reality of who we are and what we can offer. Someone I hadn't seen for a long time sat by me in church recently and said, 'I feel like a broken reed.' I know that's how I often feel and perhaps always will, and maybe God can use us 'broken reeds' as we are—thinner-skinned, conscious of all we don't know, but at the same time growing in humility and sensitivity and hence less likely to be brash, hearty and trite in the face of other people's vulnerability and suffering.

Perhaps we should find ways of letting our needs be known, and of contributing our insights and whatever else we might be able to offer. Jesus would not break bruised reeds; he came to comfort mourners, bind up the broken-hearted and set prisoners free (Isaiah 42:3; 61:1–3); and he washed dusty feet (John 13:1–15). Do any 'strong', confident, privileged, upfront people need to be made more aware of all this? Appearances may be deceptive, however: they may not feel nearly as perfect and successful as they seem! Suffering gives us all—'strong' or 'weak'—the opportunity to grow in loving wisdom and tender toughness.

'Even the saddest things can become, once we have made peace with them, a source of wisdom and strength for the journey that still lies ahead.' (Frederick Buechner)

1 PETER 1:6–7

Faith—reality checked

Now for a little while you may have had to suffer grief in all kinds of trials. These have come so that your faith—of greater worth than gold, which perishes even though refined by fire—may be proved genuine and may result in praise, glory and honour when Jesus Christ is revealed.

These verses can be interpreted to mean that God sends suffering in order to improve our character, but that's far from the only way to understand them. I remember someone telling me, 'The Lord took Mike.' I knew he meant well, so I smiled sweetly at him, but inside I was thinking, 'No, he didn't. He's got him in his safe, loving hands but he didn't take him.' I would prefer to say that God allowed him to die—that in an imperfect world of fallible people, things sometimes go wrong, as they did, for reasons as yet unknown, during Mike's operation.

Perhaps you would be happy to hear that God had 'taken' your loved one, but I had come to my own conclusions in my own time and way—and they were somewhat different ones, though faith and God were still very much involved as far as I was concerned.

'Has Mike's death shaken your faith?' a friend asked me. On that particular day I think I replied that if it had, completely, I'd have to be giving myself a hard time about it, because the kind of faith that's swept away by personal tragedy isn't really worth having.

For me, a faith for all seasons involves trusting that God is with us in our bereavement, and with us and our loved ones in death and in the new life beyond. It also involves being real about my bereavement and all life's sadness and mystery, and real in my continuing relationship with God, myself and others.

How is your faith affecting and being affected by your experiences? Is your creed and are your priorities the same or changing?

JOHN 11:25–26; REVELATION 21:4b

Grieving with hope

Jesus said... 'I am the resurrection and the life. He who believes in me will live, even though he dies; and whoever lives and believes in me will never die. Do you believe this?'

There will be no more death or mourning or crying or pain.

Canon Scott Holland wrote many helpful pieces for bereaved people, but the way he began one of them was not, in my view, helpful or even true. 'Death is nothing at all,' he wrote. Well, whatever death is, it certainly isn't 'nothing at all' either to those who die or those who grieve.

The inquest was over and a verdict of death by misadventure had been returned. In bed that night, I cried to God for some reassurance and comfort, and turned to the Bible passage for the day.

As I read the story of Lazarus being called out of the grave, I had a mental image of Jesus calling Mike out of his grave and into 'bliss', eternal life. This thought brought me comfort, along with another picture of Mike enjoying a fantastic feast in heaven—the theme of the preacher at Mike's memorial service.

The Christian hope is that our loved ones have been, and that one day we will be, called out of physical death into new life, where sadness, injustice and evil will have no place and everything will be explained and understood. With that as our big picture, we still grieve, deeply and fully, because we're human and those capacities are part of God's design for us. But we also grieve with hope, for we trust that the biggest question of all—'Was it worth it? Was the great creation adventure worth the suffering and evil?'—will ultimately be answered with a resounding affirmative from all creation.

Lord, I am grieving with hope because...

ISAIAH 43:19; JEREMIAH 29:11

Creating a life

See, I am doing a new thing! Now it springs up; do you not perceive it? I am making a way in the desert and streams in the wasteland.

I know the plans I have for you… plans to prosper you and not to harm you, plans to give you hope and a future.

The loss of our loved one has forced very unwelcome changes on us, and we can't press any 'undo last action' keys in relation to them. We can choose our responses, take stock of our lives and make good adjustments, however. Who are we now? We are the same person in many respects, but with new insights, qualities and skills emerging from our experiences. So there will be a blend of old and new in terms of our identity and capacities.

The same will apply in relation to our way of life, interests and priorities. At some stage we may have to move house—though most counsellors advise against any such big changes in the first few years. We will keep at least some old friends and make new ones. Do we need to cut down on work, or do more of it, or change to a different occupation? Do we need to make more space for leisure, friendships, reflection, creativity or exercise? Have we become aware of having lived largely reactively, responding to the urgent, constantly chasing our own tails?

How could your life and agenda reflect something of the spirit of Marjorie Hewitt Suchocki, when she writes, 'The edges of God are tragedy. The depths of God are joy, beauty, resurrection, life. Resurrection answers crucifixion; life answers death'?

Lord, I want to live as fully, lovingly, creatively and productively as I possibly can. Help me to draw on all your past and present resources in and around me, so that I can do just that in time and eternity.

Our Bible reading notes

BRF offers five different series of Bible reading notes which approach the Bible in different ways to help you enjoy reading and begin to understand the Bible's message. Which one is best for you?

New Daylight is our most popular series. The full Bible text is included. The passage is explained by one of our experienced writers, who will help readers understand the Bible passage and how it is relevant for their own spiritual journey. Available in print, Deluxe edition (includes larger print size), app for Android, iPhone and iPad and daily email.

Guidelines is for people who are hungry for a deeper study, who are ready to hear what current biblical scholarship has to say, what differing theological viewpoints may exist, and who want to make up their own mind on how the passage becomes relevant for them. Available in print, app for Android, iPhone and iPad and PDF.

You can find out more from

- your local Christian bookshop
- www.biblereadingnotes.org.uk
- BRF Direct 01865 319700

Day by Day with God provides a woman's eyes' view on the Bible. Written by women for women with an evangelical emphasis, taking account of the things that matter most to women. Available in print and app for Android, iPhone and iPad.

The Upper Room contains meditations that show real people living faithfully in real-life situations, with the Bible as the touchstone for and measure of faithful living. The meditations are provided by *The Upper Room* readers themselves from around the world. Ideal for new Christians. Available in print and PDF.

Quiet Spaces is for people who enjoy exploring the Bible using their innate spirituality and creativity. Each edition contains nine themes explored in different ways. These include biblical reflections, views on the theme from a wide sweep of Christian tradition and history, prayers and meditations and a creative activity to take the reader deeper into the theme. Available in print.

Available the way you want to read!

BRF Bible reading notes are available in a printed booklet, as an app for Android, iPhone or iPad, or as a PDF download for your laptop or PC, meaning your notes are easily available whenever that spare five minutes appears in your day!

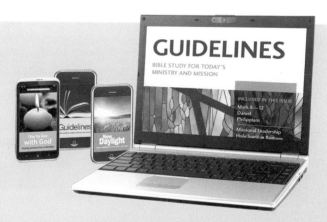

Bridget & Adrian Plass

The Apple of His Eye

Discovering God's loving purpose for each one of us

Bridget Plass

First published in 1996, Bridget explores the Bible passages which tell of God's loving purpose for each one of us, as well as for our wider communities.

pb, 978 1 84101 088 5, 160 pages, £7.99
Available for Kindle

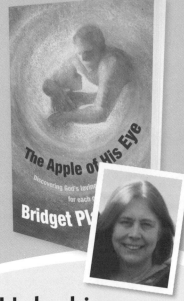

The Unlocking

God's escape plan for frightened people

Adrian Plass

The Unlocking is a book that has established itself as a Christian classic. Adrian takes you on a voyage of discovery through the Bible, exploring fearful situations—and frightened people—and reflecting on some of the many ways in which God meets you with his healing love and grace, no matter how daunting your circumstances.

pb, 978 0 7459 3510 2, 160 pages, £7.99
Available for Kindle